Snake Meets The Wizard

SIDE A - BAND 1

JOHN HARDIN

MMO 2012

Blues for Ross

Comp. Arr.
Doug Walter

MMO 2012

A Child Is Born

COMPOSED & ARRANGED BY THAD JONES

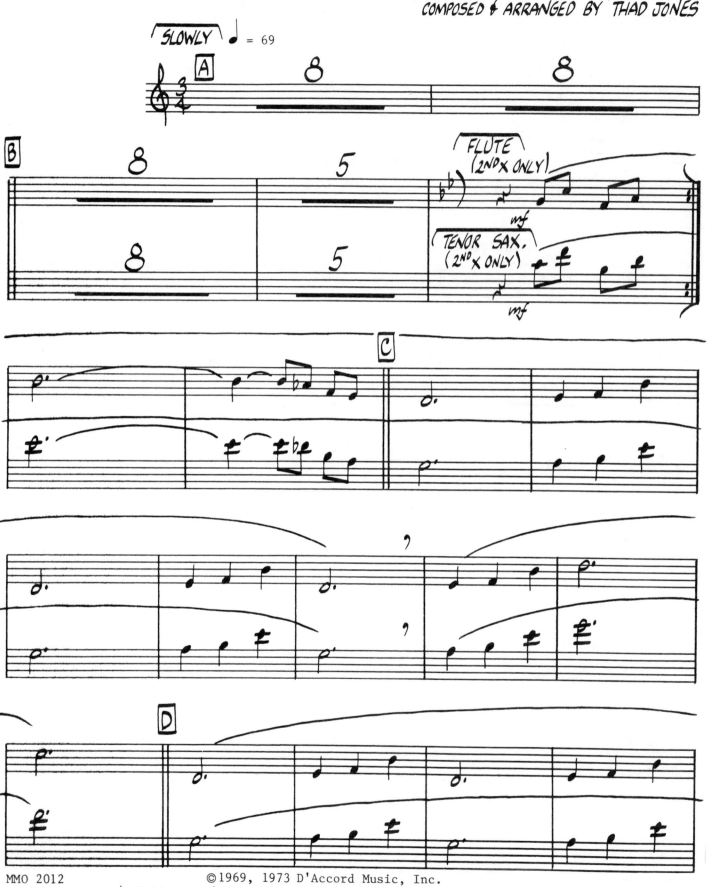

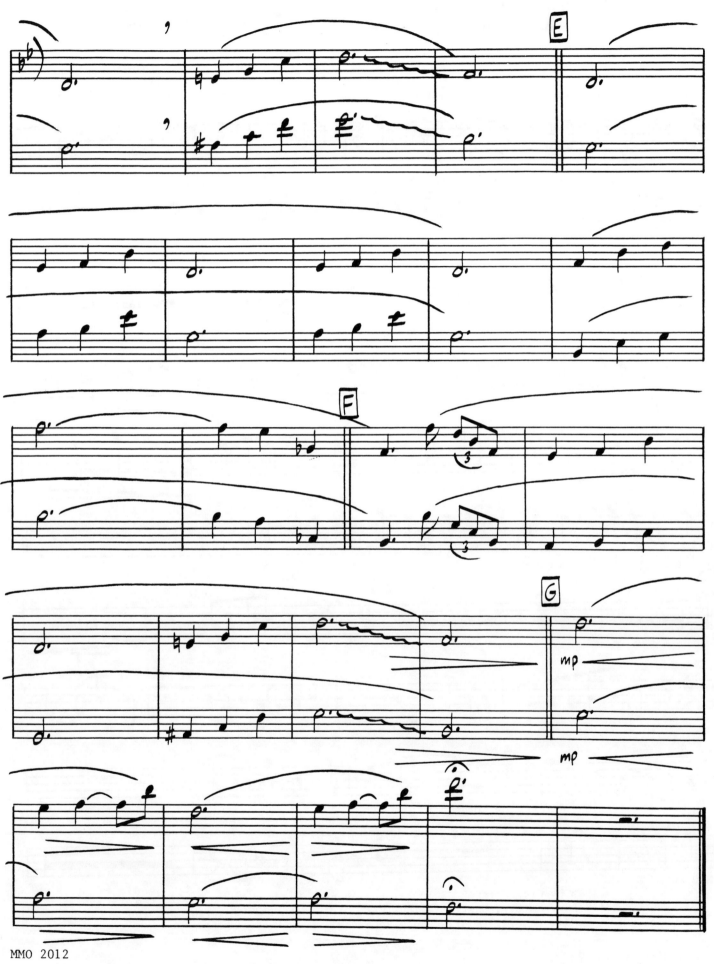

Antithetical Arsis-Thesis

SIDE A - BAND 4

COMP. ARR.
GREG SORCSEK

7 taps (1 measure) precede music. ♩ = 188

MMO 2012

Dancing Men

4-measure drum solo precedes music. ♩ = 138

John LaBarbera

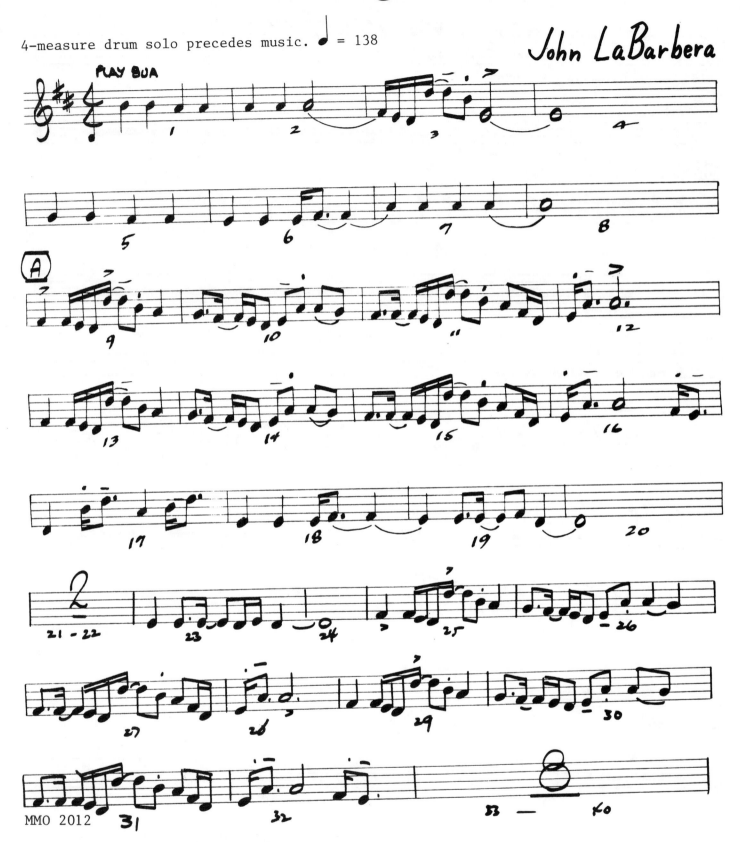

MMO 2012

14

Nice n' Juicy

4 taps (1 measure) precede music. ♩ = 100

MMO 2012

She Cries

Richard De Rosa

SIDE B - BAND 3

MMO 2012

•WORLD'S LARGEST CATALOGUE OF *Participation Records*